Plants in My World

LET'S PLANT A TREE

Marigold Brooks

PowerKiDS press

NEW YORK

Published in 2018 by The Rosen Publishing Group, Inc.
29 East 21st Street, New York, NY 10010

First Edition

Editor: Theresa Morlock
Book Design: Michael Flynn

Photo Credits: Cover Africa Studio/Shutterstock.com; p. 5 Syda Productions/Shutterstock.com; p. 6 Lori Adamski Peek/Getty Images; p. 9 aluxum/Getty Images; p. 10 Steve Sparrow/Getty Images; p. 13 KidStock/Getty Images; p. 14 amenic181/Shutterstock.com; p. 17 David H. Carriere/Getty Images; p. 18 Matthijs Wetterauw/Shutterstock.com; p. 21 KWSPhotography/Shutterstock.com; p. 22 Armin Staudt/Shutterstock.com.

Cataloging-in-Publication Data

Names: Brooks, Marigold.
Title: Let's plant a tree / Marigold Brooks.
Description: New York : PowerKids Press, 2018. | Series: Plants in my world | Includes index.
Identifiers: ISBN 9781538321201 (pbk.) | ISBN 9781538321225 (library bound) | ISBN 9781538321218 (6 pack)
Subjects: LCSH: Trees–Juvenile literature. | Trees–Growth–Juvenile literature.
Classification: LCC QK475.8 B76 2018 | DDC 582.16–dc23

Manufactured in China

CPSIA Compliance Information: Batch #BS17PK: For Further Information contact Rosen Publishing, New York, New York at 1-800-237-9932

Please visit: www.rosenpublishing.com and www.habausa.com

CONTENTS

Good for the World

Trees give people and animals the oxygen they need to breathe. They give us shelter from the sun, wind, and rain. Trees have deep roots that hold the soil in place.

Start Digging

First you need to decide where to plant your tree. It will start out small, but it needs room to grow. Once you pick a spot, you have to dig a hole.

A tree needs room to spread out its roots.
Make the hole deep, but also make it wide.
Place the tree into the hole and cover the
roots with soil. Then, pat down the soil.

9

Your tree will be thirsty after being buried in the ground. Use a watering can or hose to water your tree. The water will sink into the soil and the tree's roots will drink it up.

Trees need sunlight and water. They also need a gas called carbon dioxide. Trees turn water, carbon dioxide, and sunlight into the energy they need to grow.

Saplings Growing

A young tree is called a sapling. Sometimes it takes years for a sapling to grow up. Fruit trees usually start to grow fruits when they're about five years old.

Life of a Tree

Some trees can live for hundreds of years. The oldest tree in the United States is in California. It's a Bristlecone pine and it's almost five thousand years old!

17

18

You can tell a tree's age by counting the rings inside its trunk. A tree with many dark rings has been alive for a very long time. A tree with just a few rings is very young.

Squirrels and birds build nests in trees. Raccoons and owls live in tree trunks. Deer eat the leaves and fruit that grow on branches.

Many trees are cut down to make room for cities. Cutting too many trees harms our planet. It's very important to plant trees to keep Earth healthy. Someday your tree could grow high as the sky!

WORDS TO KNOW

sapling

trunk

watering can

INDEX